What We Found Along the Way

WHAT WE FOUND ALONG THE WAY

by Cathy R. Foreman and Mary R. Foreman

© 2025 Cathy R. Foreman
All Rights Reserved

No part of this book may be reproduced, stored, or transmitted in any form or by any means, electronic or mechanical, including photocopying, recording, or any information storage and retrieval system, without written permission from the publisher, except for brief quotations in critical articles or reviews.

Photos by Cathy R. Foreman
Map Illustrations by Shantal Rozier

Published by MaeCarol Press

First Edition

ISBN 979-8-9930292-0-7

to our HEARTBEAT 🫶

though you were not with us on our adventures, you were with us in more ways than you'd imagine.

we LOVE you... *INFINITELY*

FOREWORD

by Kecia L. Peterson

As a longtime friend of Cathy's... and of *"Ma Foreman,"* as she's so affectionately been dubbed - I've had the rare pleasure of witnessing a bond that is something truly special. In the three decades I've known them, I can honestly say I've never seen a mother-daughter relationship quite like theirs. Their connection is rooted in love but lives and breathes in friendship. They move together like old friends who've been through a thousand inside jokes, spontaneous road trips, and heartfelt moments. There's no formality - just a shared passion for life, discovery, and laughter.

I've had the absolute joy of traveling with Cathy and Ma Foreman and let me tell you - whatever you think the trip is going to be, it absolutely will not be that. That's the magic of riding with these two. You may start with a clear route and final destination in mind, but somewhere along the way Cathy will say, *Oh! We're not far from...* and that's it - she's making a sharp left, punching the gas, or heading toward an unplanned road that suddenly becomes the highlight of the journey. And the best part? You never regret the detour. In fact, it becomes the part of the trip you remember most.

One adventure that stands out in my memory is the time Cathy and I traveled to Philadelphia. Rather than taking the highway, she insisted on the scenic route - the back roads. *We ain't paying for tolls.* And I'm so glad she did. We saw an entirely different side of the city, one that most people would never experience. Rolling hills stretched out in front of us, occasional windmills spinning gently in the distance. We passed small towns that felt frozen in time, each with its own unique charm.

Contents

- Introduction
- Origin Story: How It All Began
- Castle McCulloch: We Ain't Going Back
- Berry Hill Plantation: The History We Found
- Italia: Everything and Then Some
    - Sorrento
    - Amalfi
    - Florence
- The Memphis Blues: Where We Paid Our Respects - and a Price
- PBS: What We Found on the Other Side of a Segment
- The Myrtles Plantation: The Past Still Lives Here
- Selma to Montgomery: The Distance Between Then and Now
- Pilot Mountain: We Earned the View
- Can We Get Back into the Country: The Kind of Trouble We Recognize
- Finding Your Roots: The Dirt Knows Everything
    - Africatown
    - The Legacy Museum & Lynching Memorial
- Curiosity Damn Near Jailed the Cat: We Were Almost the Story
- I Didn't Cancel My Vacation: It Was Mine to Take
    - *Holler*, If You Hear Me
    - The Cork & A Village
    - Witches, Writers and Weathered Souls
- Epilogue: To My Mom
- Closing Words
- About the Authors

What We Found Along the Way

Introduction

I appreciate books for what they are and what they offer, but calling myself a *"book reader"*? Well, that's a stretch. I'm more likely to skim the Cliff Notes or wait for the movie to drop. But give me a good article or a human-interest piece, and I'm all in.

I've always been fascinated with origin stories - where things start, how they unfold. And that's how I ended up here.

I was reading - yes, reading *(yeah, yeah, I know what I said, but I was really hyped about this book)* Love and Whiskey by Fawn Weaver when the storytelling struck a chord with me. As a journey(wo)man myself, I found pieces of my own life as the story unfolded. I couldn't help but laugh, nod in agreement, and at one point, I even found myself saying, *Girrrrl, now you know!* All the while, I was thinking, I've lived that.

So, naturally, I went to my mom and said, *I have an idea.*

Without missing a beat she replied, *Oh Lord, where we going now?*

I explained how I was reading this book - how parts of it mirrored our experiences, and how we had stories of our own that could inspire and entertain. She listened and then simply said, *Okay.*

Now, I'm not one to take her *"o - kay"* at face value, so I pressed on: *You do realize you're gonna have to be part of this.*

She grinned and in her own drop the mic moment said... *Hell, I was there. That's input a-dam-nough.*

We both burst out laughing. But the truth was, she was in - and that was the most important part.

This collection of stories... of life and laughs, maybes and maybe-nots... binds us closer as mother and daughter.

So, stick around and join us on this journey.

ORIGIN: HOW IT ALL BEGAN

Well, I told you I love a good origin story - so here we go.

This book's been in the making long before I ever thought to write it. Over the years, our travels became more than just trips - they turned into stories of connection, discovery, and, more often than not, pure hilarity. As I recapped many of our trips to friends and co-workers, a few would often ask, *Where's the book?* So, I guess they planted the proverbial seed.

What We Found Along the Way is a sample-sized collection of those stories - a record of the bond that grew between my mom and me in ways neither of us could have ever imagined. Through these experiences, we came to understand not just who we are, but how truly remarkable we are - how big of dreamers we are, and ultimately, how very much alike we are. It's our hope that our journeys resonate with every reader who delves into our journey.

It all began in 2011 when I was working at a hotel with my time split between two properties - one in Raleigh, and the other in High Point, NC. Every Sunday, my mom and I would leave Raleigh, drive the 1.25 hours to High Point, and return on Tuesday evening. Since we didn't have a specific time to arrive on Sundays, we took our sweet time. Oddly, we used to complain about those leisurely Sunday drivers, but then... we'd suddenly become those very people.

But here's where we differed - instead of staying on the main highway, we'd just-veer off. We'd follow the signs, follow our curiosity, and simply... drive.

Week after week, we started noticing the *"brown"* historical signs, road markers, and sometimes even billboards that caught our attention. If something seemed interesting, we'd go for it.

Now, because we'd be in High Point for a couple of days, we decided we should explore the town. I called these little excursions *"walk-a-bouts"*, a term I'd picked up from *Crocodile Dundee* - an Aussie thing. But really, these strolls gave us the chance to learn more about this little town, known as the *"Furniture Capital of the World."* After my workday ended, we'd head out - sometimes driving, sometimes walking around - and chat with the locals. Sometimes we'd drive just to get lost on purpose... because what's the fun in sticking to the beaten path?

And that, my friends, is how this all started. We did this for about eight months before I returned to my primary property full-time.

But here's the thing - we were hooked. And then, feeling a sense of limbo, we looked at each other and said, *Okay, what now?* So, naturally, we started doing day trips. Let me be clear - these weren't just your average two-hour jaunts. We're talking five hours or more, with no real destination in mind. More times than not, we'd make it up as we went along. We lived in the moment, letting spontaneity guide us like a map with no directions.

Friday nights, without fail, my mom would ask, *Are we going somewhere tomorrow?* And of course, I knew exactly what that meant. My answer? *Sure!*

She'd pack a bag of *"essentials,"* and we'd set a time to leave - usually around 5 or 6 AM, but never later than 7. And off we'd go.

Essentials meant a mix of practicals and why-nots. For us, that included: underwear, bottled water *(for drinking and washing)*, alcohol, toilet paper, paper towels or wipes, scissors, a machete *(yes, really)*, a Daniel Boone-esque knife, snacks, band-aids, an umbrella, and a few more things I'm probably forgetting.

Now, you might be wondering...

Why all the random stuff?

Some will get it. Some won't...

If you stay ready, you don't have to get ready.

And well... adventure always demands a little preparation. The bag is always packed - if not already in the car – 'cause if things ever go sideways *(thankfully, they never have)*, we are ready.

CASTLE MCCULLOCH: WE AIN'T GOING BACK

Some places speak louder than others. Some tell you to turn around.

Sitting in Jamestown, North Carolina - maybe fifteen minutes from High Point - is an authentic castle called Castle McCulloch. Built in 1832, the castle was originally used as a gold refinery. Later, as the gold era of North Carolina dwindled into decline, the castle was abandoned. It wouldn't be until the 20th century before it was restored and repurposed as an event center - its grandiosity now playing host to weddings and gatherings.

We'd driven past the sign for gem mining and the castle more than a few times, always noting it but never stopping. There was just something about the phrase *"gem mining"* and the word *"castle"* in North Carolina that seemed too odd not to eventually investigate.

So, one Sunday, we finally did.

Jamestown, in its ruralness, was quiet, uneventful, and unassuming - at least from what we could gather. We found the entrance and pulled in to park. As we made our way down the path toward the castle, there was evidence of a party. The path and trees were strewn with beads, streamers, half-inflated balloons-like Mardi Gras had come and gone without the cleanup. It was an odd juxtaposition.

As we walked farther, we noticed signs - literal signs.

Satan's Lair. and *The Devil's Den.*

Jagged letters on weathered boards. Odd things to see in a place where weddings are hosted. I didn't like it. I didn't like it - not one bit. Something about it didn't sit right with me.

I turned to my mom and said, *I don't know if we should be back here.*

She brushed it off. She wanted to see the castle. I sighed and followed - because this is what we do.

The castle itself was... well, stunning in its own way. A small bridge led us across a shallow moat to a pair of imposing, grand wooden doors. As we entered, we were met with hand-hewn woodwork, detailed, and heavy, and a massive two-tiered chandelier of wrought iron hung above us. Intricate carvings - lion heads and other motifs - filled the corners. It was dark and dramatic but beautifully done. The kind of place you'd expect in medieval Oxfordshire - not the backwoods of North Carolina.

What had initially drawn me to the location, admittedly, was the potential for bridal portraits. It seemed the perfect setting. But standing in the middle of it, even amid its grandeur and magnificence, something still didn't feel right to me.

We stepped out and followed the winding path that led us to what they call the Crystal Ballroom - an octagonal room encased entirely in glass. Inside were chandeliers, mirrors, and all the gaudy opulence you could ask for - but the energy in that room made my skin crawl.

I didn't linger. I walked in and walked right back out.

Mom stayed.

Normally, I was the one who lingered in places like this. But today, something in me couldn't bear it and said *Nope!*

By the time she caught up with me, I was already making my way back toward the car.

I didn't say much at first - just kept walking. But the farther away we got from the castle, the heavier everything felt. I couldn't shake the feeling. Something was undeniably off...

but what exactly?

I'd never felt this kind of weight before. And it made me uneasy in a way

I couldn't explain.

I told her, *We need to get off this property. I don't feel right.*

We climbed into the car, closed the doors, and as I reached for the ignition, a sudden impulse stopped me. I turned to my mom and said,

We need to pray.

So, we did - right there in the parking lot.

We asked that anything that wasn't ours to carry - anything dark or strange - be left behind and not follow us off that land. That no picture or memory tries to hold on where it wasn't welcome.

I don't think Mary took me seriously. But I was dead - ass - serious.

Then we left - but fast.

Once we reached the hotel, I took out my camera and just started deleting every single photo I had taken at the castle. Every - last - one.

Then I said another prayer over the camera, asking that any trace of that place be wiped clean - gone for good.

And that was the end of it.

We hadn't spoken about Castle McCulloch until now. By the way... Mary is still laughing at me, but guess what?

We haven't been back.

And - we ain't going back.

Berry Hill Plantation: The History We Found

History doesn't hide. It waits.

Illustrations by Shantal Rozier

It was an event for wedding vendors. One of those early days in my photography era when I was still figuring out my lane. The DJ, whose name I can't recall, struck up a conversation with my mom. She told him about our spontaneous road trips - how we were always in search of the next best place to explore. I think she mentioned our visit to the Myrtles Plantation. *(When I asked her about it for this book, she gave me a classic "I-don't-know" look, heavy on the attitude).* Anyway, that's when the DJ told her about *Berry Hill Plantation* in South Boston, Virginia - a place with ruins of stone slave quarters.

That was all we needed to hear. History? Plantation? Road trip - Let's go!

It was in November and Veteran's Day weekend when we decided to make the trip. I can still picture all the flags and patriotic decorations that dressed the town for its annual celebration. That town felt like a time capsule - postcard-esque. So, as we always do, we drove around to see what hints of nostalgia and history it had to offer.

Once we were out of the town, the backroads started to narrow, and houses grew sparse. *Over the river and through the woods*, we joked. Thank God we were driving early in the morning. After a while, we finally saw the sign for the *Berry Hill Entertainment and Conference Center.* It certainly didn't scream historic. We were confused at first, thinking, *Surely, this can't be the place.*

We pulled over to double-check Google Maps when a good samaritan stopped to ask if we needed help. We explained we were looking for the plantation with the slave quarters. He confirmed that yes, the slave quarters were indeed on the property we had passed. So, we hooked a u-ie and headed back.

When we finally entered the drive, just over a crest, we saw the ruins -

three stone slave quarters standing tall but dilapidated on either side of us. Both excitement and chills rushed over me. But something about it didn't seem quite right. Was this it? ... Right here at the road? ... Right here - in our faces? I had expected them to be hidden, tucked away from public view, but there they stood - unguarded - unapologetic. It just didn't feel like that was all there was. I thought there had to be more. So, we kept driving.

We drove further up the path, passing the *"Big House"* turned Conference Center and saw all the tell-tell signs of preparation for an event. So, we parked - to be out of the way and to see if there was actually anything else to see.

That's when we noticed a sign for *Diamond Hill Cemetery*. 1.5 miles ahead, it read. Little did I know Diamond Hill is the largest slave burial site in Virginia, with over 300 unmarked graves.

In that moment, it didn't matter what else we saw - we had to go there. The only issue? We couldn't drive down the path.

In my head, 1.5 miles didn't seem like a big deal. But when you don't know where the hell you're going, 1.5 miles can feel like 10. Regardless, we set off - ever the adventurists. We walked down a dirt path, hills rising here and there. Eventually, we found ourselves surrounded by vast fields, with nothing in sight but random pieces of old and rusted farm equipment.

Then, a sudden realization hit me: I - had - to - pee!

Stop laughing! Well, go ahead and have this laugh on me. Listen, I'm a country girl, and squatting in the woods? Not an issue. And Mary, my mom - well, she is the original MacGyver, always prepared. She handed me tissues, and I was good ta-go. Just as I was about to squat, I made sure not to get my jeans wet, so I came out of one leg. That's when I looked up and saw my mom,

snapping away

taking photos of her *"naked-ass baby"*

in the woods.

That's exactly what she said. We couldn't stop laughing. It's one of those stories we'll laugh at forever and I can't believe I'm including it in this book.

Business taken care of, we pressed on. I walked ahead, as Mary - now cuss'n me – asked, *how much farther we have to go?* I yelled back, telling her I could see a clearing. Maybe we were close. So, she kept following me.

At the end of the path, we came to a fork in the road.

To the right? The cemetery.

To the left? Who knows?

What do you think we did?

The unknown got the better of us and we went left. And thank God we did.

Down the path, we discovered two more stone slave quarters. Five in total, including the three by the front. We walked through them, trying to take in the enormity of it all. These quarters were made of stone... stone! Not wood like what we have been programmed to believe - and they had massive fireplaces used for cooking and warmth. The fireplaces were so large, an average-sized person could almost stand in them. They even had multiple rooms, which was practically unheard of for slave quarters.

As we touched the stones, trying to imagine who lived here, how many people slept in these rooms, we were left with questions.

Why were these quarters stone?

Why were they so far from the Big House?

It was sobering, humbling, but we moved forward. The next dwelling we found was in worse disrepair than the last.

By now, my curiosity had the best of me. I was determined to see the cemetery. I asked my mom if she wanted to come, but she told me to go ahead and fill her in later.

Now, remember, we were way back in the woods - no cell service, no one knew where we were - and I ventured out alone - leaving my mom to her own devices.

After a good piece of walking, I called back to Mary, but all I heard was the rustling of leaves as the wind blew through them. Still, I pressed on. Eventually, I reached a small hill, where a white sign read, *"Welcome to Diamond Hill Cemetery."* Behind it, a large tree stood with a cross made of two small limbs leaning against it. My heart started to race.

I entered the space, but what I found shocked me. No headstones. Nothing. The area was full of trees, but no markers, no graves - from what I could tell. It didn't make sense. I pushed forward, thinking maybe I'd find something hidden deeper in the brush. But all I found were slight indentations in the ground - barely noticeable. Not the kinds of things you'd recognize as grave sites - if you were unaware. I even sat down on some fallen trees, trying to process that this was a slave burial site with no visible markers. I was puzzled - angry, even. How could this be?

Now, I understand that you might be asking, *Cathy, did you really expect* to find something?"

And the answer is - *Yes!* Yes, I most certainly did.

I wasn't in the habit of visiting cemeteries... past or present. So, I had no concept of slave cemeteries being unmarked, and my logic was, if it's advertised - if it's known - there should be something there.

Right?

But I was wrong.

As I sat there, I reflected, then stood up and continued walking. It wasn't until I neared the edge of a slope that I saw something peeping through the leaves - a small stone - a plaque - inscribed with these words:

> "In silence,
> We remember and regret.
> The chains are gone
> Though windswept trees
> Whisper forever your fate.
> Rest in Peace."

I walked back; a bit disappointed but at peace with what I'd experienced. I thought I'd have to completely backtrack to find my mom, but instead, I met her at the fork. She said if I'd been any longer, she'd have come looking for me. I told her what I had - or rather hadn't - found, and she simply said she'd see the photos.

We started our trek back to the car. Back - up, down and over those seemingly long 1.5 miles.

As we approached nearer to our car, I spotted another cemetery. While mom proceeded to the car, I wandered over. This one - full of markers of the families who once owned the land and, therefore, the enslaved who were forced to exist on the property – as a part of the property.

Back in the car, we headed back to the front of the property and stopped at the last quarter, the one closest to the road. I walked through this one, though I hadn't gone into the two others.

As I stood in the kitchen, looking through a small opening in the wall, I caught a glimpse of the *"Big House."*

Something about that view unsettled me.

Then it hit me.

"They" could see everything - every move this enslaved family made.

They were watching... and the inhabitants, the enslaved, were always under surveillance.

I couldn't shake the question: *Why were these quarters out front, while the others were buried deep in the woods?*

And today, I still don't know the answer, but I've never forgotten that realization - being watched.

That morning was filled with laughter and humility - holding space for both.

What We Found Along the Way

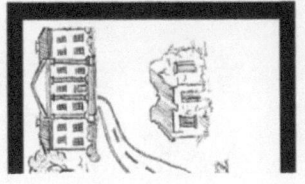

Berry Hill Plantation

South Boston, Virginia

ITALIA: EVERYTHING AND THEN SOME

Some journeys begin with a map.
Ours began with a deep breath and too many damn bags.

Okay, so technically, this wasn't a road trip in the sense that we've shared thus far - but it sure felt like one.

In 2011, my world shifted. A life altering event hit me square in the chest, and all I could think about was going to Italy. I was ready to book the next flight, come hell or high water. But one of my friends - calm, rational, annoying in that wise way - talked me down. She said I needed to wait until my head cooled and I could actually plan the trip I truly wanted. I didn't want to hear that shit at the time, but she was right. And I didn't go - that time.

Fast forward to 2013. I started plotting the real trip. And of course, my road dawg was in. She was 100% on board. We gave ourselves a year to save and plan. The travel agent handled flights and hotels - as for the rest? That was all me.

Now, if I haven't mentioned it before - maybe I have - we don't do tours. Hate 'em, actually. We don't like being herded around or on someone else's clock. Rush here, snap a picture there, keep up with the group. Nah! We wanted to move slowly, soak up the moments, immerse ourselves in the surroundings, meet people, get lost on purpose. If this was going to be our only chance to see Italy, we were going to make it count.

Two weeks. Milan. Florence. The Amalfi Coast. Go big or stay home, right?

Side note: I fell in love with Italy as a kid watching the soap opera As the World Turns. There was a fictional family called the Grimaldi's - wealthy, dramatic, with scenes filmed on what they called the "Grimaldi Coast." For decades, I believed it was an actual place.

When I finally started researching the trip, I searched for what I knew - The Gramaldi Coast. It kept returning - Amalfi.

I was confused as hell.

Turns out the Grimaldi Coast was fiction (go figure), but Amalfi? That place was stunning.

Our plan was to fly into Milan, take the high-speed train *.Italo* down to Naples, base ourselves in Sorrento for a few days, then double back to Florence, and finally return to Milan for our last leg. I didn't realize how tightly I'd packed the schedule until we were in it, but Mary, as always, was down for the ride.

I'm skipping the flight details because nothing really interesting happened. Just the usual: cramped seats with not enough leg room and the people in front of you not caring that their seat is in your lap as they fully recline.

But let me tell you, I thought I had done all the research - best travel season to avoid tons of tourists, train schedules, everything. I even bought our train tickets in advance to lock in times and reduce surprises. We'd taken care of almost everything stateside so once there, it was just food, souvenirs and any attractions.

We packed like we were leaving the country for six months instead of two weeks. Two big 28" suitcases, a 20" carry-on, oversized shoulder bags, my camera gear and laptop, and Lord knows what else. But we were ready.

We landed in Milan - midday. And y'all - that luggage?

We were immediately humbled. Walking long distances with all that weight was a struggle.

Clearing customs was no joke either, but somehow, we made it through and headed to the train station. I was genuinely relieved to see train signs in English - didn't expect that - but bless the folks responsible for that decision.

Now here's where things got shaky.

At that point, I'd only been on a train once - when I was fourteen. So of course I misread the boarding screen. The terminal had no lifts, and we lugged everything up to the wrong platform. We even sat down thinking we were good. It wasn't until I rechecked the board that I realized my mistake.

When I told Mary we had to go back down, cross over, and climb back up - with alllll that luggage - the look she gave me could've melted steel. Cuss'n the entire way - she did it. I took my 28" and all the smaller bags so she could focus on her suitcase alone.

She almost made it. Al-most.

Near the top of the stairs, she tripped. Fell up the steps. *(I know, a clutch my pearls moment for sure.)* Her suitcase went flying back down to the bottom. I rushed to her aid, fearing the worst, but she said she was okay. Down the stairs I went to grab the suitcase while she sat there bruised, pissed, and a little tickled. Thankfully she wasn't seriously hurt. But oh, she cussed me out like I'd set her up. We'd been in Italy for less than four hours, and my name was already mud.

We finally made it onto the train, where we had to separate from our luggage, required to maintain the open seats for passengers. I didn't like that one bit. Every time the train stopped, I kept eagle eyes on that luggage rack. I made Mary sit as close as possible. If anything happened to those bags, I - would have - NEVER - heard - the end of it.

As we moved through the countryside, I couldn't help but notice the scenery. Open fields, farmland, towns with beautiful pastel-colored homes, and graffiti - so much graffiti. I hadn't expected that.

We arrived in Naples early into the night and realized the local train to

Sorrento had stopped running, but I had done all the research - side-eye. So, we grabbed a cab - €140 for the hour-long ride. Pricey, but what choice did we have?

The cab driver was kind and tried pointing out landmarks, but it was so dark, we couldn't see a damn thing.

When we finally got to the hotel in Sorrento, the front desk handed us this bulky but mini doorknob-esque room key - that would prove to be much too much to take outside of the hotel. Charmed and not too tired, we checked in, freshened up, and decided to explore. We set out for the city center, about 15 minutes away on foot, but turned around halfway. Basically, we said forget this.

We spotted a restaurant right next to our hotel - thank God.

Now, remember how I said I'd done all this research? Another side-eye. Well. We sat down, ordered our meal - pasta, steak, wine - and when the bill came, I confidently handed over U.S. dollars.

The manager blinked.

We don't accept, he said.

We sat there dumbfounded - with our cards in the room, and money unconverted. We tried to explain. He listened, then waved us off.

Come back tomorrow, he said with a smile - ushering us out with our glasses of wine.

We left in shock.

Did that just happen?

We asked, without saying a word. He'd trusted us - two American strangers - on our word.

Who does that anymore? Clearly, in Italy - they do.

Back in our room, we showered, rinsing off 24 hours of travel, confusion, laughter, and a touch of humiliation.

Sorrento, the next morning

We woke up the next morning and stepped out onto our balcony –

and there it was –

Mount Vesuvius, rising in quiet majesty across the water.

Breathtaking. Stunning.

Honestly, I still don't have the right words for what it felt like to stand there, seeing it in real life. Everything around us felt like discovery - a new country, new sights, a view so beautiful - that it left us speechless.

We were basking in the reality of where we were.

So naturally, we did what any two giddy travelers might do:

stood on that balcony and yelled "Ciao, Italia!" into the breeze,

and laughed at how corny we sounded.

Pure perfection.

Downstairs, breakfast was a feast - a sprawling spread of scrambled eggs, fresh fruits, muffins, pastries, prosciutto, figs, dates, and cheeses. Everything looked too pretty to eat. As Americans used to a basic continental breakfast and lukewarm hotel coffee, this felt luxurious.

Beautiful. Abundant. Delicious.

We took our time, savoring every bite.

Afterward, we set off to find the Piazza Tasso, the city square we hadn't quite reached the night before. On the way, we passed the restaurant, where the manager had kindly let us dine without paying, telling us to come back tomorrow. Only now, it was closed - we'd have to settle up later that evening.

Further down, perched just above us, we stumbled upon a lemon grove. We climbed a small set of stairs and entered this little haven where the smell of lemons hung thick, permeating the air.

Sweet. Sharp. Fresh.

We sat on a couple of wooden benches and let our senses catch up. That's when we noticed they offered homemade limoncello tastings. Interesting. Now, I was pretty sure Mary wouldn't partake - she didn't drink. *(wink-wink)*

At the back of the grove, there was a tiny stand - something like an adult lemonade stand, complete with fresh lemons, old-fashioned pressers, and bottles of limoncello ready for sampling or purchase.

We got our little cups and found a seat. I watched as Mom took a sip - and her face just lit up with this wild pucker. It was hilarious. She let out a Nature Boy Rick Flair *"Wooo!"* and smacked her lips like she'd bit a lemon straight off the tree. I couldn't stop laughing. I had to get it on camera.

When she went in for a second sip, I was ready - not sure if she'd react the same way, but I couldn't risk missing it. And sure enough, she did. Whether it was genuine or for my entertainment, I don't know - but I got the footage. Too funny.

I always joke that the only time she drinks is when we're in another country. So far, that still holds.

Leaving the grove, we made our way into Piazza Tasso, the city square I mentioned earlier. We wandered, eyes wide, still in awe that we were actually in Italy. Though we were still full from breakfast, we peeked at menus posted outside of restaurants - such a nifty thing, being able to scope out your options before stepping inside.

Still, we weren't ready to eat again just yet. That's when we spotted a little "tour train" heading down toward the marina. At first, we brushed it off - until we peered over the edge and saw the long, winding road leading down. It looked like it never ended.

So, we changed our minds, bought tickets, and hopped aboard. The train had audio guides in several languages: English (UK), Spanish, French, and more. We listened, looked, and quickly took in the sights - spiraling down to the marina and back up again. The whole ride was quicker than expected. Nice, but not nearly enough.

So, we did what we always do - went back to do it our way.

But first... lunch. A cashier at my pharmacy had told me, *You must get linguine vongole when you're in Amalfi.* And ba-by, I did. Linguine with baby clams in a lemon and caper sauce. So simple, so fresh - but My God. It was divine.

After lunch, we were ready to take on the spiral again - this time walking, on our own time. We marveled at the hill's height, at the carvings and niches tucked into the stone.

Let me be clear - this wasn't just a hill - this was a mountain. As we made our way down, bend after bend, we were gifted with new angles of the sea and the inland cliffs. Constantly reminded of God's power and man's craftsmanship. The awe never wore off.

At the bottom, we wandered into a small cathedral and said a prayer of gratitude. Then we browsed a couple of shops, took a moment for gelato, and found a bench in Piazza San Antonio.

People-watching.

Gazing out at the sea and Mount Vesuvius again.

Inhaling it all.

I also remember the cats. An absurd number of them gathered near the square - lounging, prowling, unbothered. I'm not a cat person, so I kept my distance, and they thankfully returned the favor.

We didn't linger long, though - we still had to make the trek back up that mountain.

We went the way we came and never thought twice about the steep metal stairs bolted precariously to the side of the mountain. A steady stream of folks shuffled up and down, but something about those rattling steps hanging off all that rock just didn't feel safe to me. Ugh, no! - Hard pass.

By the time we reached the top, night had fallen. We made our way to the restaurant from the night before, and sure enough, the manager greeted us with a knowing smile.

I knew you'd be back, he said.

We laughed, paid our tab - and decided to stay for dinner. Thank God the hotel was nearby.

Amalfi, Positano, Ravello. Florence. Milan. Each with their own story - but some are better told over a shot of limoncello and some linguine vongole. For now, I'll just share a few short vignettes.

WHAT WE FOUND ALONG THE WAY

Sorrentini Lemon Grove

What We Found Along the Way

Amalfi - what a gorgeous coastline

One of the most unforgettable things about Amalfi - aside from the stunning coastline - was the drive. I know, I know... you're probably thinking, *Really?* But hear me out. That drive was utterly insane.

We were in a 15-passenger van, winding our way along a mountain that clearly was so narrow - it seemed too absurd for any type of large vehicle to be on. These curves weren't just curves. As Mary put it, they were *"deep-ass curves"* that, while allowing for some of the grandest views, made you question gravity and life choices. Our driver? Cool as a cucumber. Clearly a seasoned pro of this winding madness.

But then we hit this one curve.

A massive tour bus - massive - was coming around the bend from the opposite direction. And let me tell you, it was way too big for this two-lane cliffhanger of a road. Everything ground to a halt. Our driver threw it in reverse, and soon everyone behind us had to do the same.

It was intense. Harrowing doesn't even begin to describe it - at least not for the folks on our van. For the locals, though? This was just an ordinary day. Business as usual. They were already out of their cars, fussing, waving arms and helping to direct traffic like it was nothing. Nobody blinked.

All the while, we were inching backwards on a sliver of road carved into the side of a mountain like we were trying to un-pour water from a glass. Meanwhile, everyone in our van was plastered to their windows, eyes wide, probably praying in at least three languages watching this sight unfold.

Then - because of course - out of nowhere, a moped materialized. It zipped in and out between the tightly packed vehicles like it had a death wish.

A collective gasp burst from the van. Someone might've actually screamed *JESUS!* - it might've even been me; I can't be certain.

And just like that - after what was probably only a few minutes but felt like forever - the tour bus cleared the bend. The road opened up again. We all exhaled in unison, shoulders unclenching, hearts gradually returning to their regularly scheduled programming.

And we kept going. Like it never happened.

Another side note: Some time later, I was watching TV at home and caught The Italian Job, the original - 1969 version - with Michael Caine. There's a scene where he and his cohorts were on one of those huge buses, flying around the bends of Amalfi - almost like that bus was on my trip but there was no one else on the road with them. And watching how they took those curves took me back to that moment... all I could say was, "Hell naw!"

Amalfi Coastline

Florence - where friendships are born

Mary told me there was no way I could write about Italy and not include Florence. After all, it's where we met our dear friend Khalil.

We wandered the city, circling the Duomo, the Cathedral of Santa Maria del Fiore - a must-see. The entrance doors, cast in solid brass, have weathered into a deep patina over the centuries. They stand as more than doors, really - one monumental sculpture made of many smaller ones. In one vignette, believers have rubbed Jesus's foot so often that the brass gleams through. The entire cathedral is like that, a composition of countless details within the magnificence of the whole. Inside, the grandeur - tempered by simple elegance - holds even more artistry, layered with the soft echo of whispers as visitors pay the space its due respect.

If you're facing the Duomo, we headed off to the right - the side with the tower. That stretch is alive: street artists, musicians, little shops bursting with color and character. It's the kind of place where the air hums with creativity.

We stopped to watch a street artist, Kahlil, sketching a tourist. I struck up a conversation with him, and we hit it off immediately. I took a few photos of him while he worked, and when he finished the portrait, we kept chatting.

He asked to see the pictures I'd taken, and as I flipped through them, he caught sight of some of my art. That sealed it. We were kindred spirits.

He pulled out his phone to show me some of his own work. Next thing I know, he's closing up his stand - asking his artist friend, next to him, to keep an eye on it - so he could walk with us and treat us to a coffee.

He pointed out a couple of places we had to see and even walked us to the ticket office. We ended up visiting the Accademia, where we stood before Michelangelo's David, and later wandered over to the Piazza della Signoria beside the Uffizi Gallery, where we took in the open-air sculpture gallery in reverent awe.

The next day, we returned to sit with him again. This time, he sketched my mother. I remember sitting behind him, watching his hands bring her to life on paper. My eyes welled up. She was having a moment - her moment - and it moved me deeply to witness it.

Every time we return to Italy, we make a point to stop in Florence and see Khalil. Outside of that, we stay in touch on WhatsApp, swapping photos and little updates about our lives.

A friendship born on the streets of Florence - kept alive across oceans.

THE MEMPHIS BLUES:
WHERE WE PAID OUR RESPECTS — AND A PRICE

Even sacred ground can leave a scar.

We were in Nashville, Tennessee, for the Music City Jazz Festival, where I had the honor of creating the souvenir flyer artwork and photographing the event. Afterward, being so close to Memphis, we decided to venture out and visit the historic *Lorraine Motel*.

It was a good three-hour drive from Nashville to Memphis, and while we had the time to make the trip, the whole trip was a whirlwind - a blend of the music festival, an unexpected detour to Hurricane Mills, and then Memphis, where we had to call the police. By the end of it, the term *"Memphis Blues"* took on a whole new meaning.

We left Nashville in the early afternoon. After a weekend drenched in off-and-on torrential rain, the drive felt like a welcomed reprieve. Music on the radio, the open road ahead, and billboards catching our eye: one for Tina Turner, another for Loretta Lynn. I'm a fan of both, but I couldn't resist the pull of Loretta's homestead, especially since I missed an opportunity to visit Butcher Holler, her childhood home featured in *Coal Miner's Daughter*, during a trip to the Kentucky Derby years before.

We turned off the main highway and followed the signs to Hurricane Mills. The road led us six miles away from the main thoroughfare, until we reached what they called the *"homestead."* There, we found cabins - simple and sturdy, reminiscent of early homesteads. Picture *1883* - the kind of home Margaret and James Dutton might have built, or like the cabin in the pilot episode of *Little House on the Prairie*. We walked through them, snapping photos, exchanging stories about growing up country and some of the tools and such, reminiscing about simpler days.

But there had to be more than just these cabins, right? I couldn't shake the feeling that we hadn't seen everything.

We drove on, down a dusty road, further into the countryside, until we found the tiny town of Hurricane Mills... Loretta's own sanctuary. It was picturesque - complete with a water wheel, a replica of the coal mine her father had worked in - complete with coal, and her Butcher Holler home, a post office, small shops, an Arrowhead Museum, and the crown jewel: the home Doolittle Lynn built for her. If you've seen *Coal Miner's Daughter*, you know the scene where Loretta tells Doo she doesn't want the *"dadgum"* bedroom at the front of the house because the sun would shine right in her eyes every morning. Can you tell - it's one of my favorite movies?

Though we couldn't tour the home (*we were now pressed for time - burning daylight*), it was a delightful stop, and I was as happy as could be.

Back on the road, we finally made it to Memphis. Pulling up on a side street near *The Lorraine Motel*, I wasn't prepared for the neighborhood. Honestly, I was a little apprehensive about the area, not ever imagining that this would be where we'd find this piece of history.

The Lorraine Motel - like all civil rights landmarks - was poignant. We bought our tickets, and from the moment we stepped inside, we were transported into history. The exhibits were thoughtfully curated, impactful, and told the story of preceding events leading to Dr. King's assassination. There were moments I couldn't help but feel a lump in my throat, but nothing hit quite as hard as the *"I Am A Man"* exhibit - honoring the garbage workers' strike, the Rosa Parks bus protest, and the Freedom Riders bus bombing exhibit. The intensity of each exhibit grew as we moved through them.

But it was the Rosa Parks exhibit that truly gripped me.

I never imagined having the reaction I did. From the moment I stepped onto the bus - the back, of course - it hit me. My body tightened, like I could feel the weight of this history upon me. And when I sat down *(what did I do that for)* and heard the voice of the bus driver saying the words - calling her nigger - I became enraged. I couldn't get off that bus fast enough.

I had to pull myself together - remind myself where I was... what *this* was. An exhibit, yes, but one so real it cut straight through me. And there was so much more to see.

We moved on through the exhibits, listening to recordings, soaking in the heaviness of the past. And then, we reached room 306, the room where Dr. King had stayed - the very room where he had been moments before his assassination.

Spoiler Alert

In the hallway leading to the room, the mood is somber and heavy as Mahalia Jackson's *"Precious Lord"* is pumped through the sound system. The weight of what's to come - palpable.

In the glass-encased exhibit, we stood just outside of the rooms where Dr. King and his team had stayed. The faded remnants of their lives were displayed: hair pomade, open and faded milk cartons, napkin-covered plates on the side tables, and indentations where they had rested on the bed. It was a time capsule, frozen in a moment that changed the world.

When we exited the space and the hotel, we ended up in the gift shop. Unaware of *"Part 2"* of the exhibit, our cashier asked if we had completed the tour. Of course, we said *yes*. And it was then that we were informed about the boarding house across the street - the boarding house where James Earl Ray had stayed - watched - and ultimately fired the fatal shot, killing Dr. King.

It was another one of the most emotional experiences of my life.

Every item in that room - every detail - told the story of the man who took away an icon. His underwear. The beer packaging. The rifle. Even the windowsill that still held the indentation where Ray had rested his tripod. It was almost too much.

Everything they pulled from the room for the investigation had become a part of the exhibit. Even the point of view from the bath, also encased in glass.

I maneuvered to get as close as I could, and as I stood there, I could see exactly what he saw: the balcony where Dr. King stood moments before his life was stolen.

As we left the exhibit, we were solemn. There were no words, just the quiet weight of the day.

We walked back to the car and drove to our hotel. Instead of settling in, we needed to shake off the intensity of it all.

So, we ended up on Beale Street - at BB King's - for a great meal and some incredible live music. Later, we took a stroll down Beale Street and even hopped into a horse-drawn carriage to catch a glimpse of downtown Memphis.

Drained, we returned to our room and called it a night.

The next morning, before heading back home, we decided to swing by Graceland. Not really my thing, but it was there, so we stopped by since we were there. We didn't tour the mansion - *we're not fans like that* - but we did visit the museum across the street, housing Elvis' plane and some other memorabilia.

Back across the street and beside the mansion was a souvenir shop. So, we parked against the wall that separates the two properties, walked around to the front of the mansion, and signed the *"remembrance wall,"* adding the name of one of our dear friends, Agnes, who's a huge Elvis fan. Then we went inside the shop and bought a few trinkets.

And then - it happened.

Walking back to the car, I noticed some miscellaneous items strewn on the ground - outside of the passenger door. It didn't register at first. We got in and headed out. Down the road, about to get on the interstate, my mom reached for her bag... she pulled out nothing - it was gone.

Frantic, we pulled off the road into a subdivision to check the car. Still nothing. And then we noticed that there was something else missing - an entire suitcase.

In utter disbelief, I tried to get my mom to remember what all was in the bag so that we could make some phone calls and place holds on everything. Of course, her driver's license, her social security card, a couple of credit cards, and my FSA card. So, I called all the cards to place holds on them and to request new ones. Thankfully, they had not yet been used.

As for my FSA card, well, the idiots clearly didn't know what it was, as they tried to make a $80 purchase at Sonic. Yes, that Sonic - the burger joint. Dummies!

Having taken care of as much as we could, we went back to the souvenir shop, asking if they had footage of the parking lot. They did, but the clerk had to call the manager. In the meantime - we called the police.

When the officer arrived, she was very nice and sympathetic with us. Then we learned that the camera footage was useless.

Trying to recount everything that was stolen, that's when it hit my mom - the missing suitcase was the one we purchased in Italy and inside were a few newly purchased A-line bras. Not cheap by any means.

That set her off and she muttered ...

Sorry som'bitches. I hope their assholes burn like fi' when they shit. I worked too damn hard for my shit. No one has the right to take it.

Even now, when talking about it, she gets riled up and pissed all over again. Memphis holds no good memories for her and owes her - at its very least - her A-line bras.

She swears she'll never go back, and if we ever find ourselves needing to go that way again, we damn sure better go around Memphis, according to her.

And so, that, my friends, is *The Memphis Blues*.

PBS: What We Found on the Other Side of a Segment

*Some places speak your language,
even if you've never been there before.*

There's a little gem of a show on PBS called *North Carolina Weekend*, hosted by Deborah Holt-Noel. Deborah travels across the state, uncovering hidden gems - restaurants, attractions, and activities - that you might never hear about, depending on where you live. It's the kind of show that makes you rethink the places you pass by every day, turning your backyard into an adventure waiting to be had.

For us, *North Carolina Weekend* became the unofficial guide to our early road trips. My mom, Mary, kept a running list of destinations she wanted to explore, though I didn't know it at the time while I had my own list - but it never felt quite as curated, more a collection of whims.

One evening, mom pointed out a segment about Bostic, a small town in the western part of North Carolina, home to a quintessential country store called Washburn's General Store. If you're wondering where Bostic is, we felt the same.

It's essentially in the middle of nowhere - the middle of nowhere - but to us, that was part of the allure. It felt like we were about to embark on one of our favorite pastimes: backroad adventures.

Washburn's reminded us of Tillery, where we grew up - a rural town that, like Bostic, you could miss if you blinked. On a Friday night, Mary casually suggested we visit the country store. The next morning, we were up at 6 a.m., on the road with purpose and a destination.

Now, let me tell you, when I say Bostic is in the middle of nowhere, I mean middle of nowhere. We wound our way through countless small towns, each with its own rhythm, adjusting our speed for every little town line.

Along the way, we passed murals, vintage cars, and little window displays that whispered, *stop and see me...* while abandoned houses stood as quiet, forgotten witnesses to time's passage.

Finally, we arrived at Washburn's. Stepping inside felt like stepping into a time machine. The exterior of the store was brick, not wood as I had imagined, but inside, the shelves were packed with vintage and replica goods that immediately transported me back to the early '80s in Tillery.

There were two things that drew us in. For me, it was the size 72 dungarees - jeans, as we call them now. For my mom, it was the elevated train track that ran the length of the store.

We both found joy in the small things - giggles escaped as we whispered to the trinkets, *come here, come here*. Each item was a little portal to another memory.

This store had everything you could think of for a rural community - items I'd seen on retro TV shows, like the ones my grandmother and I used to watch together.

My mom, meanwhile, was downright tickled as she recalled using certain tools with her father - on his farm. It was one of those rare moments where everything felt right, and we simply reveled in the nostalgia of it all.

We didn't just shop; we soaked in its history. Washburn's had been around since 1831 and has been owned and operated by five generations of Washburn's. It was even listed as a nationally registered historic site.

As an extra treat, we met Edward Washburn III, the eldest living member of the family. He sat on a pew in the middle of the store, watching the comings and goings like a living, breathing piece of the place's history.

With a Pepsi in one hand and a nab in the other, he chatted with everyone who crossed his path, embodying a kind of vintage charm that only a place like Washburn's could produce.

I could almost hear the nostalgic clink of peanuts being dropped into a Coke bottle - an echo of my childhood.

When we left, we were both full of that quiet joy only travel can give you - the kind that comes from discovering something unexpected. But there was still plenty of daylight left, and we weren't ready to head home just yet.

True to form, we started driving, unsure of where we'd end up next.

As fate would have it, we saw a sign directing us towards Chimney Rock, about 1.5 hours away. So off we went, setting course for the next chapter of our spontaneous adventure.

To get to Chimney Rock, we must pass through Lake Lure. Beautiful, and serene, we stopped at the hotel and walked around the property – admiring the view of the lake just across the street.

Suffering from drought, the lake had receded, jagged and sparse, yet it somehow still enhanced the beauty of the area. Later we found out this was the filming location for *Dirty Dancing*.

Then on to Chimney Rock - known for its hikes, but we opted out this time, instead strolling through the charming little shops on Main Street. One store looked like it had been lifted straight from *The Andy Griffith Show* - a couple sat in the window, playing checkers as if the world outside had slowed to their pace.

We smiled at the scene, the kind of unhurried moment that felt like a small blessing.

There, too, an old rusted red Coca-Cola chest, the kind where you had to slide the top open and reach in to grab a drink, using the built-in bottle opener on the side. I loved that.

We finished our day at a homemade ice cream shop, sitting on a bench, people-watching and soaking in the moment.

By the time we headed home, the day had slipped by in that way only the best road trips can.

The Myrtles Plantation: The Past Still Lives Here

Some stories don't fade – they follow you home.

On one of our trips to New Orleans, we decided to visit *The Myrtles Plantation*. I had first seen it on the TV show *Unsolved Mysteries*. It intrigued me - even more so when some years later I saw it on one of those *"haunting"* shows I used to be obsessed with. Back then I was deep into ghosts and spirits and anything unexplained. I'd done a little research: It's supposed to be one of the most haunted places in America, and of course, it was a plantation. That alone meant the ground had stories it hadn't let go of.

There's a sorrowful story tied to the place about Chloe, an enslaved house servant punished for eavesdropping. The punishment... one of her ears was cut off; she later wore a headwrap to cover the dismemberment. The version I heard said in an attempt to show her value and ingratiate herself to the family, she laced the owner's children's food with white oleander, thinking she could *"save"* them later. She miscalculated - the children died, and because she couldn't save them, they blamed her. She was hung from a tree on the property - the same tree that was still standing the day we visited.

They say Chloe still haunts the place. Sometimes on the porch. Sometimes peeking around the corner buildings. And they say the children never left either – visitor's claim to hear them or see their tiny handprints, especially on the beds. Marks of lives cut short.

So, on this particular trip, since we had a few days in New Orleans, we decided to take a day trip - about two hours away, across Lake Pontchartrain, into St. Francisville. When we arrived, we simply walked the grounds first - wanting to get a feel for the place before doing anything else. The land was beautiful: Spanish moss and massive cedar trees framed the property - beautiful and eerie like nature had signed an NDA with history.

In the back of the property, cabins that had been built more recently for overnight guests who wanted to tempt the night. You could even book a night in the main house itself if you really wanted the full experience.

The grounds... also said to be haunted - by soldiers, maybe Confederate, maybe not. Guests have claimed to hear gunshots and laughter filling the air near those very cabins. We walked through those spaces too. And like I said, at this time in my life, I was really into the haunted stuff. I was geeked. If there was something to see, I was gonna see it.

It stood in stark contrast to Castle McCulloch, where the space itself carried a rather uncomfortable edge. But here... nothing.

Not in those moments, at least

We eventually bought tickets and went on the tour. The house itself was stunning - old, heavy with history. The kind of place that doesn't creak, it sighs. Right when you walk in, there's this massive mirror in the foyer - gold-framed, antique, real ornate. They said no matter how much you clean it, there are stains - dark, permanent smudges - thought to be where the spirits of the children are trapped. The blotches - they were there.

We weren't allowed to go upstairs during the regular tour - that's reserved for overnight guests. But they told us that at the top of the stairs, people have captured orbs - those little flying balls of light - on their cameras. So, I took pictures. Of course I did. I snapped a few photos of the stairs and didn't look at them again until we got home.

One of the parlours had this gorgeous marble fireplace and velvet furniture - everything still intact, preserved. The wallpaper was light - delicate, probably hand-painted like *Gracie* paper *(thank you Magnolia Network - Home Work)*. When we got to one of the bedrooms, the guide pointed out a tiny bathtub in a corner of the room. I mean tiny by today's standards. Me and Mary looked at each other like, lady, please. That tub, perched on a stand could have held a toddler - maybe a prepubescent but certainly not a full-grown adult. But the guide told us women in that time were small-framed, petite. I couldn't imagine them being that damn small though.

She also mentioned that sometimes the children's handprints appear on the bed. She said it like it was nothing. Just... matter-of-fact. Sometimes they show up. Sure!

As the rest of the group started to walk out, me and Mary hung back - like we always do. We like to linger, take things in longer than everyone else.

And that's when it happened.

Right there on the velvet bedcover, two small handprints appeared. We saw them with our own eyes. I don't know if there was some kind of gimmick or sleight of hand - if they had sensors or something built into the bed - but I saw them. Clear as day. And it freaked me out a little. Okay, a lot. I was into all the spooky stuff, but seeing it in real life? That's different.

That marked the end of the tour.

We stepped back outside, walked around the grounds again with fresh eyes. Took more pictures. Sat on the veranda for a bit - in rocking chairs, letting the stories settle. Then we went into the little shop, bought a couple of things, and chatted with the folks working. They gave us even more history - details that weren't part of the tour, little pieces that made the whole thing feel heavier. Fuller.

When we got back home, I finally went through the photos I'd taken. And those shots of the staircase - where they say you might catch orbs? I had snapped a series of rapid-fire pictures from the exact same angle, standing in the exact same spot. But in each one, the light shifted just slightly. Like something was moving and it wasn't me - I. did. not. move. The angle didn't change. But the light did.

It reminded me of when we were kids and we'd get a stack of paper and draw stick figures on every page, flip through it, and it would look like they were dancing.

That's what it was like.

Each picture, the light changed just enough to make it feel like something was... alive.

Like something was waiting there.

Watching.

I don't know where those pictures are now. I've looked for them. Maybe it's better they're gone.

But I definitively remember and know what I saw.

From Selma to Montgomery:
The Distance Between Then and Now

This road was paved with courage - and shadowed by ghosts.

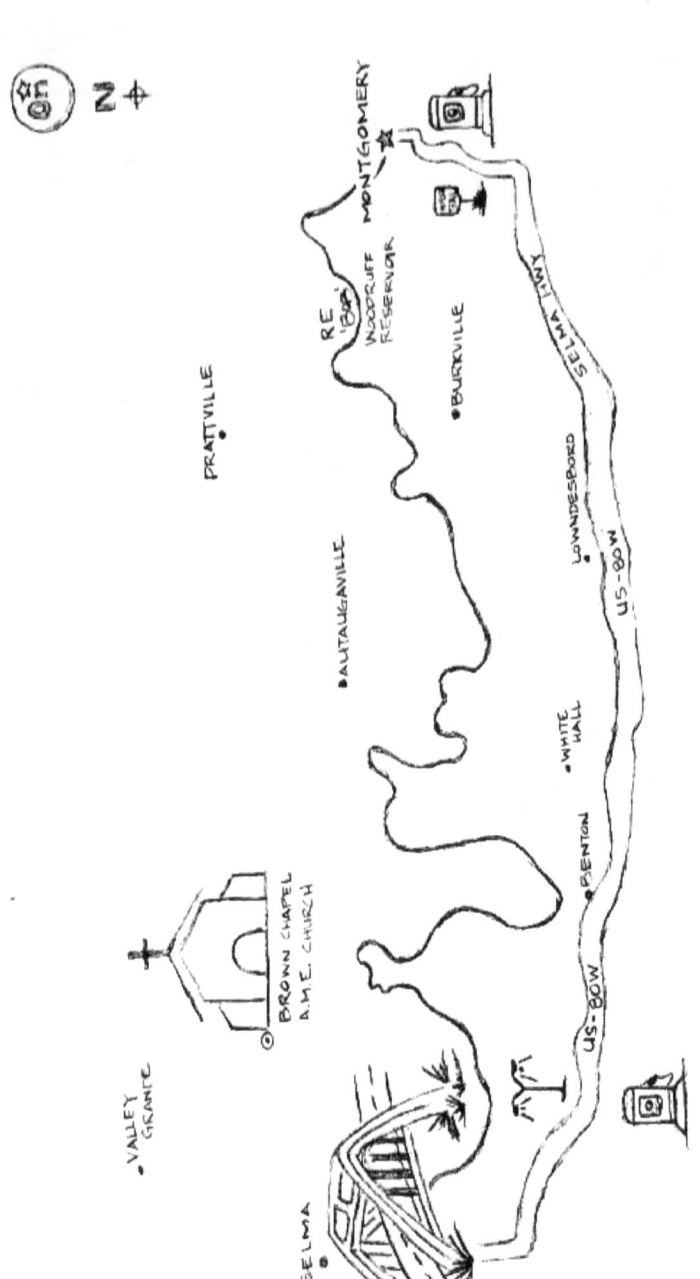

Illustration by Shantal Rozier

By the time we reached this point, we had already learned and experienced so much from our travels. But nothing could have prepared me for what was about to unfold.

On a separate trip to New Orleans - we'd driven there twice before - it was about 2 or 3 in the morning when I realized we were making great time, so much so that we'd arrive at our hotel long before check-in. And then I had a brilliant idea, like I always do - lol, let's detour to Selma so we can see the *Edmund Pettus Bridge*. I mean we were already in Alabama.

This was a short while after the 50th anniversary of the Selma to Montgomery marches.

At that time, we had OnStar as our navigation system. So, I hit that little blue button to place the call. The customer service agent was pleasant but unfamiliar with the bridge. So, while she paused to look up the information, I decided to provide some insight on the significance of the bridge and what came to be known as *"Bloody Sunday."* She seemed receptive and thanked me for the history lesson, just before setting our course.

We drove on, and soon enough, we saw the brown historic sign that read something like: *"This Way to the Historic Trail."* We followed it, and in a short stint, we started on the trail.

54 miles from Selma to Montgomery - where SCLC leader Hosea Williams and SNCC leader, the late John Lewis had attempted a peaceful march in protest of the brutal killing of Jimmy Lee Jackson, a demonstrator who had been killed while trying to protect his mother from a nightstick beating.

As we began, there was a gas station not far from the start of the trail. It seemed so ordinary and indescript in the grand scheme of things.

But that gas station would come back to haunt me.

You have to remember, it was the dead of night - darker than dark. Like O-dark-thirty, to be exact.

As we drove deeper into the trail, I couldn't shake the scene from the movie *King:*

Around the three-hour mark, Miss Viola Liuzzo, a mother, wife, and activist from Detroit who had simply refused to look away, was shot twice and killed by Klansmen on this very road. Her passenger, Leroy Moton, a young Black activist, with instincts enough to survive had slipped beneath her lifeless, bloodied body, holding his breath and his nerve.

Waiting.

For those men and death to pass him by.

It was then that the gas station crept back into my mind.

The only sign of civilization we had seen in as many miles. Its distance from us, with nothing but emptiness ahead, made me more uneasy.

I sat up straighter, my grip on the steering wheel tightening to the point of **white knuckling.**

There was absolutely nothing - no streetlights, no houses, no businesses.

Just endless darkness.

All I could think was, if it's this dark now in 2015, how dark was it in 1965?

Meanwhile, Mary is leaning over checking the gas gauge, making sure we have more than enough gas. I can still hear her as she said, *I ain't getting out pushing shit* - a sentiment she almost always says if it even remotely looks like we're running low.

This only fed my anxiety. I kept glancing at my rearview mirror, half-expecting headlights to appear behind us.

I knew it was 2015, but hell, I also knew we were not so far removed from a time when it was a thrill and sport for some others to find people like us on this long desolate road.

And there were those still today who would've found nothing more satisfying than a repeat of history.

The fact that no one - not no one - except OnStar - knew where we were, compounded the eeriness of the moment.

As we neared the end of this 54-mile stretch, just like when we started, there was a gas station. Then, suddenly, lights.

Civilization, thank you Jesus! with hands raised in gratitude for his traveling mercies.

It was raining now as we took a left turning into town. We soon crossed the bridge, and the amber streetlights gave the town an obscure, almost eerie glow at 3 a.m. We parked on a side street near the bridge, hoping the rain would let up so I could snap a few photos.

It turned out it was early enough for the paper to be prepping for its morning deliveries. We sat, watched, and waited - which, in hindsight, probably made us look like we were *"lying in wait."*

Finally, there was a break in the rain, and I ran out to take my photos. In the drizzle, I stood dead center, absorbing the history of the space, snapping away as my camera clicked in echo of the silence, the rain running over me, offering a small mercy that allowed the weight of it all settle without crushing me.

I vividly remember not wanting to get back on the road, at least not quite yet - in the dark. The thought of those 50+ miles back to Montgomery felt heavier than before. The uncertainty, the apprehension, it all weighed on me.

I kept wondering:
Has anyone been watching us?
Will we be followed back?
Do we have enough gas?
Do we need to use the restroom?

As all of these questions swirled in my head - there was one thing I knew for certain...

We were not stop'n for a muh'fuck'n thang!

Sounds paranoid, right? But, given everything, it felt more than plausible.

We got back on the road - dark, desolate, historic - and my anxiety was as high as it had been when we first left Montgomery. Somehow, though, as is often the case, the return trip was faster than the departure.

Before I knew it, we'd reached the end of the trail. The tension that had gripped me slowly loosened, leaving behind a quiet reverence for dark history. So, we continued driving to New Orleans.

PILOT MOUNTAIN: WE EARNED THE VIEW

Some days you say yes and you just don't stop walking.

It started like most of our best adventures do - with boredom. I needed to get out of the house, and the mountains, as always, were calling. Once we cleared the edge of Durham County, we decided on Pilot Mountain. We'd been there before, but only to the Little Pinnacle. This time, though... this time, we were tackling the Big Pinnacle.

The weather was just right - not cold, not hot. And more importantly, not snake weather.

We set off on the trail, not quite knowing that the terrain ahead was going to be, well, questionable. What we thought would be a casual climb turned into a real test of knee joints and coordination. The trail was littered with boulders that passed for stairs, each one as high as the bottom half of your leg. Mom, shorter than me and nursing bad knees, had to get creative. And, truth be told, I wasn't exactly skipping up them myself.

The whole scene was comical, especially once I got a few steps ahead. Other hikers, seeing her alone, would stop to ask if she needed help, like she'd wandered out of a tour group and had gotten lost. Keeping my eyes on her and always checking that she's okay, I double back, catch her up, and then get ahead again - just for the cycle to repeat itself. This is how we hike. Hell, who am I kidding, this is how we travel. It works for us. Not so much for other people.

Naturally, at some point, Mary started cussing me out. That's how I know she's still good. I honestly believe our trips wouldn't be half as fun if she wasn't swearing under her breath *(and over it)*.

We pressed on, inching up and around, stopping to rest and wonder aloud, *How much farther?* But we were determined to make it around the "*cap*" - come hell, high water, or one too many elevation changes. If it took us all damn day, so be it. We were doing this. Together.

Eventually, we reached what I assume is just below the cap, not quite the tip top, but just under. That was a whole other hike we knew better than to attempt. But there, nestled into the mountainside, were large flat and jagged boulders that created cozy nooks perfect for sitting, catching your breath, and snapping a photo or two. The view into the valley from there was something else - lush and sprawling.

We paused, sat in silence, and took it all in. It hit us - we were standing relatively close to the spot you could see from the highway. How many times had we driven past Pilot Mountain, pointing it out like giddy schoolgirls at the sight of it? How many times had we stood at the Little Pinnacle, looking across, pointing at the tiny moving dots that were hikers on the Big Pinnacle, certain we would never be those people? But here we were.

After a short rest, we rounded the bend. One of my favorite things about being in the mountains is how just a few steps can completely change your view - same mountain, entirely new scenic beauty. It's why we always find our way back to them. They're our solace.

Finally, we made it around the bend. Another beautiful view. Another quiet victory.

But now came the return. Back the way we came - up, down, over, and through.

Surely this would be easier - It was not.

Going down somehow felt more treacherous. The rock steps seemed deeper, and the side paths slicker than they had been on the way up. But with a few more expletives and a steady stream of laughter, we made it back down collapsing on a bench at the end of the trail, just sitting there, marveling at what we'd done.

The Big Pinnacle was no joke - definitely an enormous step up from the little one.

And with bad knees and all, we conquered it.

As if the mountain needed to give us a parting gift, on our way back to the car, we ran into something not so ordinary but something I sort of expected - an older gentleman standing with his pet llama.

Yep, a llama.

People stopped to take pictures, pet it, and offer it sugar cubes. I'd seen this man before, on a separate trip with a girlfriend, so I let Mom have the moment this time and she was all in - feeding the llama, smiling wide,

and

just barely dodging a lick to the face. Lmao

I could have warned her, but nope - she needed the full experience. Just like I had.

What We Found Along the Way

Pilot Mountain, NC

CAN WE GET BACK INTO THE COUNTRY:

THE KIND OF TROUBLE WE RECOGNIZE

There's a thin line between a road trip and a headline.

A few days before our birthdays - we're July babies, and I was actually my mom's birthday present, born the day after her - anyway, I decided we should go to Canada. Doesn't sound too complicated, right? Except this was during Trump's first presidency, when border control was more of a gamble than a guarantee. Entry, re-entry... all those details suddenly had weight.

I was at work when the idea hit me, so I called my mom to see if she was game. And of course, she was.

Next step: could we actually do this? And more importantly, could we get back?

I asked a co-worker, knowing he was from Buffalo - but he didn't have much to offer except a shrug and a *"should be fine."* He did, however, offer his family's contact info in case we ran into any issues and needed help.

So, I did what I do best: research. I dove headfirst into Google, skimmed travel threads, official government pages, and even called the Canadian embassy.

The verdict? If we drove, all we needed were our birth certificates and a photo ID. That was great considering Mary had misplaced her passport - but the birth certificate loophole was a win.

Now, getting back into the U.S.? That answer took a few transfers and one final, confident *Yes* from someone official-sounding. Still, I wasn't sold. So, I waited a few hours, called again, and got the same answer. Still a little leery, but we were going to roll the dice.

A few days later, we packed our *"essentials"* bag and hit the road. We based ourselves in Buffalo and checked into *The Curtiss*, a new boutique hotel with just the right amount of swank.

After settling in, we headed to Niagara Falls - just a 20-minute drive. We got there at dusk, right as the area started to come alive.

I hadn't done much research on the Falls. We were winging it, truly. Walking around, taking in the sights just before it got too dark, we noticed a pedestrian sign that simply read: *"Canada"* with an arrow.

We paused. We looked at each other.

There was a full-body turnstile ahead, like the kind at a stadium or amusement park. No guard. No scanner. Just a sign and some spinning metal.

"Wait... can we just walk into Canada like this?"

Confused as hell, we hovered near it. On one hand, we were curious. On the other, we had very vivid images of being stuck on the other side, trying to explain to U.S. border patrol how we stumbled into an international incident. Our Southern Black survivalist instincts said *keep yo' ass over here*. So, we did just that - stayed put.

What we didn't know - because it was pitch dark - was that there was a customs office right there behind some black glass. Since it was dark, and because we didn't know, it just didn't sit right with us.

Borders are supposed to be secure, right? Even though this one actually was - we just didn't know it.

So, we kept our asses firmly planted on this side -

in the good ol' U.S. of A.

We settled for the night's light show over the Falls, which was spectacular. Then back to the hotel we went.

The next morning, after an indulgent breakfast buffet, we set off for the border - just ten minutes away, but there was already a long line, drug-sniffing dogs, the works. Eventually we reached the booth, handed over our documents, and just like that, we were in Ontario - secretly praying we'd make it back just as easily.

Toronto was a two-hour drive, and we made the most of it. We drove around surveying this rich and culturally diverse area before parking and walking, exploring, and taking in the *CN Tower*.

There's a glass floor near the top, and while some kids thought it was fun to jump up and down on it, we were not amused. We got our happy asses off that glass - real quick.

We also saw folks doing a sky-walk - tethered to the edge of the building, leaning forward with the confidence of people who apparently lived life on the edge. I asked my mom if she wanted to try. She looked at me like I had five heads.

When she saw it was the equivalent of a strap keeping them from plummeting, she yanked my arm and said, *Hell naw. Brang yo' ass on.*

We ate poutine, took our obligatory photo in front of the giant Canada letters, and then headed back to Buffalo.

Now, if you think we took the same route home, you haven't been paying attention. We followed signs toward Niagara and ended up stumbling on a small aqua park where we got to see a natural whirlpool. Still in Canada, we took an air tram over it.

The roar of the water was something else - so loud it seemed to vibrate your whole body. The water was so impossibly blue, with white crests spinning into a fury. We crossed and came back. It was over in a blink, but how exhilarating.

Then we stopped to shop before deciding it was time to return, making sure not to forget our Canadian maple syrup.

Back at the U.S. border, we were definitely holding our collective breath. Angst doesn't begin to describe the moment. But all was smooth - they waved us through with no problem. That collective exhale felt like landing a plane after flying through turbulence.

We returned to the U.S. side of Niagara Falls and watched that beautiful light show once more.

Then back to the hotel we went - grateful.

CN Tower, Toronto, Ca

FINDING YOUR ROOTS: THE DIRT KNOWS EVERYTHING

Every name we remembered was a name we carried forward.

This trip came about through a convergence of two events: an episode of *Finding Your Roots* - Season 4, Episode 9, *"Southern Roots"* - and the grand opening of the *National Memorial for Peace and Justice and the Legacy Museum* in Montgomery, Alabama. It started small with a re-airing of a beloved show. Then it moved to me standing in a cemetery that was folding in on itself, staring at a name I'd first heard on television. And ending with me standing in front of one of the most evocative exhibits I had ever experienced: a collection of soil samples.

Southern Roots

The episode aired in December 2017 and featured Amir "Questlove" Thompson. I didn't catch it until a few months later on a re-air. In the episode, Dr. Henry Louis Gates Jr. delivers a gut-punch revelation to Questlove - one that left me stunned as well. At first, I assumed he already knew this part of his ancestry, as profound as it was. But he only knew a small portion of what was about to unfold. He was just as shocked as I was.

Here's the backdrop: In 1860, a schooner called the *Clotilda* arrived in Mobile Bay carrying 110 kidnapped Africans – trafficked, smuggled and forced into slavery. This ship holds the hideous distinction of being the last known vessel to bring trafficked Africans to American soil. This was more than 50 years after the transatlantic slave trade had been outlawed, and the journey itself was the result of a bet. Timothy Meaher, the ship's owner, haughtily wagered he could defy the law and smuggle human beings into the country.

And he did.

For more, the Netflix documentary *Descendant* is a must.

That history hooked me. I fell into a rabbit hole of research. Days later, I came across Zora Neale Hurston's *Barracoon: The Story of the Last "Black Cargo."* It chronicles the life of Cudjoe "Kazoola" Lewis, the last known survivor of the *Clotilda*. I thought - wait, this is what *Finding Your Roots* was talking about? But Zora had the full story or close to it.

I won't pretend I finished the book. Remember, I'm not a long-form reader. I tried, but Zora's authentic retelling of Mr. Lewis's dialect was difficult for me to parse. Still, I learned about Africatown - the community founded by the *Clotilda* survivors - and added it to our list of places to visit.

A Quick Word on the Legacy Museum

In late April, news of the opening of the *National Memorial for Peace and Justice and the Legacy Museum* hit my radar. My IG feed was flooded with images and videos from the week-long celebration - Black celebrities posting and reflecting. My mom and I had already visited a few civil rights museums, but this one felt different.

The first thing that struck me was the soil collection - actual soil gathered from lynching sites across the country. I had never heard of anything like that before. The idea of standing on ground where such atrocities took place, then kneeling to scoop that earth into a jar - that hit hard.

But what really pulled at me was the Memorial itself, often referred to as the *Lynching Memorial*.

The structure rises with massive, rectangular metal slabs - each one etched with the name of at least one victim of lynching and their county origin. They hang like specters, impossible to ignore.

These weren't abstract symbols of suffering.

These were tangible representations.

Names.

Lives.

A history too many try to forget.

I needed to see that. I needed to both stand with it - and sit with that.

Headed to Alabama — Africatown

The Memorial Day weekend was coming up - perfect timing for a road trip. On a Friday morning, my mom and I packed up and hit the road. The drive was 18 hours with our usual scenic and snack-fueled stops. We bypassed Montgomery - keeping south to Mobile.

Africatown was our destination.

We drove right through it and didn't even realize. We saw a mural of the *Clotilda* - I thought it was just public art, not the marker it would turn out to be. We kept going until something didn't feel right. *Was that it?* my mom asked. I remembered reading about a *"Welcome to Africatown"* sign, but we hadn't seen it. Sure we had gone too far, we looped back, and there it was - across the street from the mural.

We stopped, took photos, then drove deeper into the neighborhood.

Africatown felt forgotten.

Not empty, just heavy. Like a whisper of something sacred. Some homes were tidy and well-kept. Others were collapsing in on themselves. My mom said, *I hope no one's living in those.* But we knew better.

We saw elders on porches, an older gentleman piddl'n in his yard in that particular way Southern elders do - more meditation than chore. A sign on one property caught my eye: *"State-acquired due to unpaid taxes."* I couldn't help but wonder - who will claim this history next?

We circled back, to where we started, where the elders remained. As we pulled into their driveway, we were greeted like family. Instantly, I was transported to my grandmother's yard – her hand waving and welcoming as guests pulled into our driveway.

We met Miss Bernadette, Miss Sarah, and Miss Edwina. They told us what remained: a church with a memorial to Cudjoe, the mural and the hill above it where a chimney once stood, and a cemetery. But no artifacts, no buildings from the original *Clotilda* days. Time had taken them.

We also met Karliss Hinton, the great-great-grandson of Fannie Keeby, one of the Africans smuggled on the *Clotilda*. He was a character - funny, vibrant, unforgettable.

After chatting for a bit, we needed to get back on the road. But Miss Bernadette offered us a bit more respite and directed us to her son's restaurant, in downtown Mobile - *Kazoola*. Yup, you guessed it - a tribute to Cudjoe, their ancestor.

Before heading there, we went searching for the other spaces they had spoken of. We found the church, perched on the edge of town like it had been waiting. Outside stood a bust of Cudjoe - proud and unmoving. We climbed the hill above the mural. W remained of a chimney rose there, alongside a small concrete post etched with the name *Meaher* - a stark reminder of his reach.

Later research confirmed it. The land had been purchased. From Meaher, of course.

Across the street was the cemetery - wild, sunken, crooked. Headstones slumped, their names weathered and smudged by time. In the middle of it all - a single obelisk. Cudjoe's grave... ringed with tributes - coins, flowers, and an empty bottle. And right beside it, like a punch to the gut, was a new cemetery - immaculate, bright, orderly.

That, too, felt like part of the story:

the taking

the replacing

the forgetting

Africatown moved me. It was hard to reconcile the sacred weight of the place with how little of it had been preserved. But I shared that space with my mother, and I won't ever forget it.

What We Found Along the Way

What We Found Along the Way

The Legacy Museum and the Lynching Memorial

We arrived the next morning around 8:45 a.m. The Memorial was enclosed, adding a quiet anticipation to everything. As we waited, I felt stillness settle in.

Once the gates opened, the first thing we saw was a series of sculptures by Ghanaian artist Kwame Akoto-Bamfo - seven life-sized figures chained together, each one carved with such humanity and pain that you couldn't look away.

They were devastatingly beautiful.

Next came the path up to the hanging sculptures - each one etched with the name of a county and the names of known lynching victims relative to each.

You begin face-to-face with the sculptures, but as you make your way through the exhibit, they rise higher and higher – until, eventually, you're standing beneath them.

And suddenly, you're in those old photos - looking up at history's ugliest truth.

I remember the silence. A few whispers but nothing more... the kind of silence that demanded that type of respect.

I searched for Halifax County, where I'm from, and Wake County, where I live.

I found them.

The sculptures seemed to stretch on forever, each one a quiet shout from the past – an insistent reminder that *I. Was. Here.*

The Legacy Museum pulled us deeper. I only wanted to see the soil collection. That's what had drew me.

We found it, spotlights shown down like they were illuminating memories themselves. Jars of earth, each one labeled by name, place, and date - a haunting, poetic reclamation of forgotten lives.

It was beautiful.

It was devastating.

And it left a permanent mark - something I certainly couldn't turn away from.

I came back from that trip heavier, yes - but also clearer.

I understood in my bones that remembering is a form of resistance.

That silence has a cost.

And that the story - our story - is still being written.

National Museum for Justice and Peace – Montgomery, AL

What We Found Along the Way

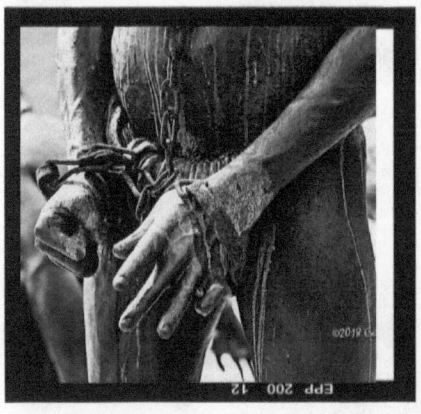

FOR THE HANGED AND BEATEN.
FOR THE SHOT, DROWNED, AND BURNED.
FOR THE TORTURED, TORMENTED, AND TERRORIZED.
FOR THOSE ABANDONED BY THE RULE OF LAW.

WE WILL REMEMBER.

WITH HOPE BECAUSE HOPELESSNESS IS THE ENEMY OF JUSTICE.
WITH COURAGE BECAUSE PEACE REQUIRES BRAVERY.
WITH PERSISTENCE BECAUSE JUSTICE IS A CONSTANT STRUGGLE.
WITH FAITH BECAUSE WE SHALL OVERCOME.

▷ 1 ▷ 2

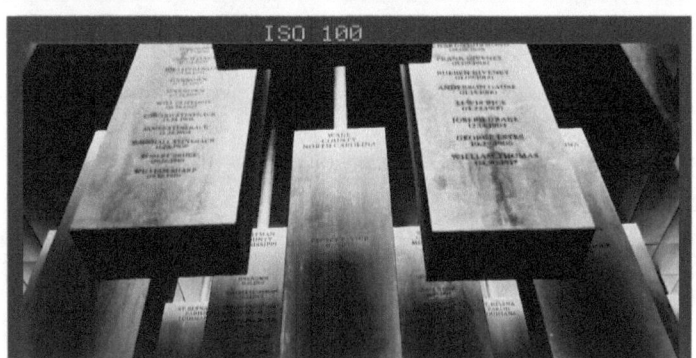

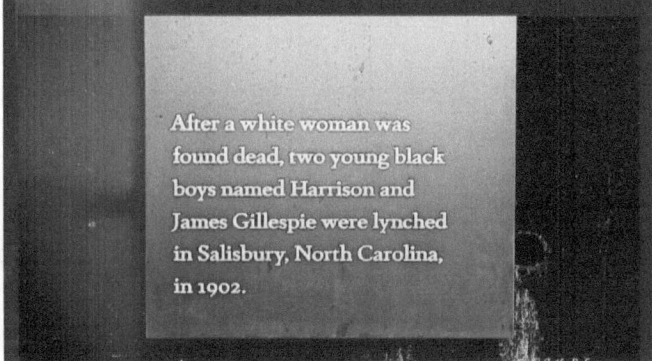

CURIOSITY DAMN NEAR JAILED THE CAT:
WE WERE ALMOST THE STORY

Sometimes curiosity is a gift.
Other times, it's just barely not a misdemeanor.

What We Found Along the Way

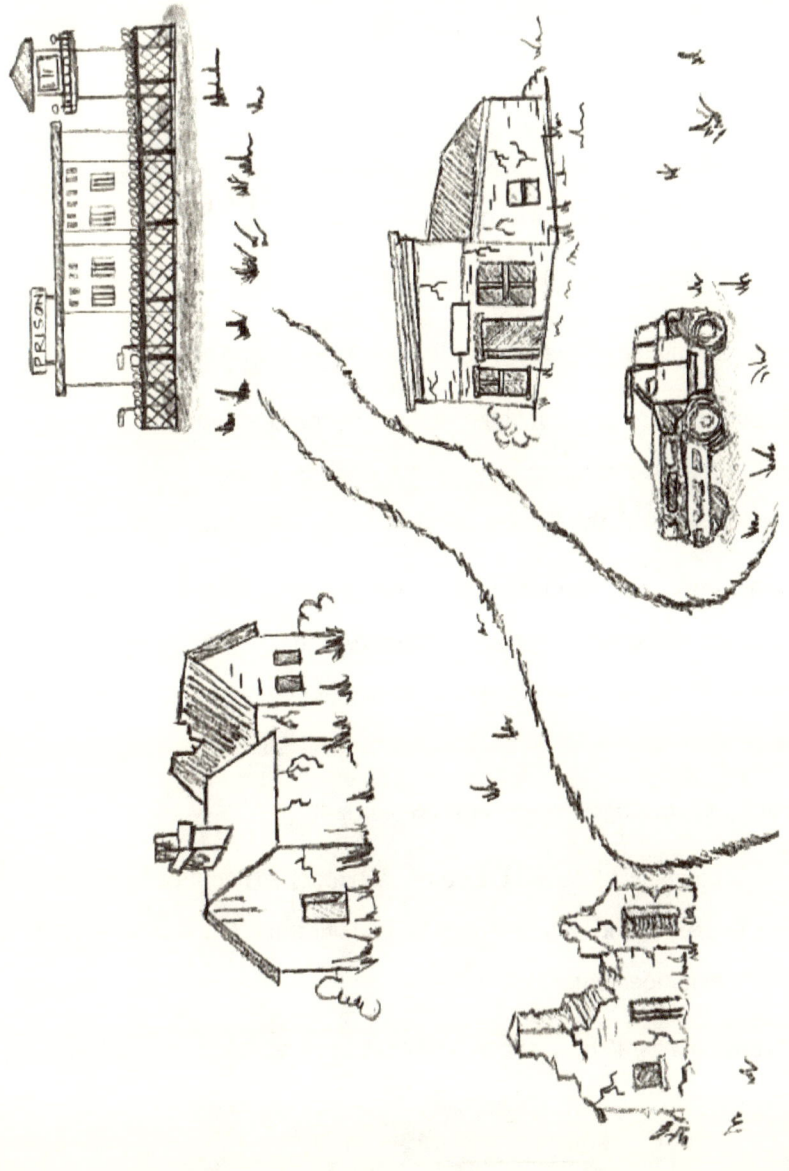

illustration by Shantal Rozier

Picture rural New York - rolling hills, open pastures, and wind turbines scattered like giant pinwheels across the horizon.

I was fascinated. Up until that point, I'd only seen solar farms stretching over acres. Never a windmill farm.

We were taking the back roads, *(as we do)* just cruising along, when I saw this old building that looked like a long-forgotten post office.

Abandoned. Crumbling. Asking to be explored.

So, of course, we pulled off just enough to hook a u-ie and rolled into the lot.

I hopped out, camera in hand. Mary stayed in the truck, probably already sighing inside. I wandered up to the building, peeking through dusty windows, pressing my lens against the glass to catch whatever the shadows left behind.

There were a few other empty buildings nearby, and curiosity took over. I walked, through high grass, standing on fallen rock just to get me high enough to peek inside, shot, wandered some more firing of photo after photo – lost in my little exploration.

Then I heard the rumbling of rocks - tires coming fast.

A police truck came flying around the corner and stopped hard near me. At this point, I was already making my way back toward our truck, thinking I was done, when the officer jumped out.

What are you doing here? he snapped. *You can't be here.*

I blinked. *Why not?*

This is a prison.

I looked around, confused. *No... the prison is over there - behind the fence.*

He didn't laugh. Instead, he stepped closer, clearly annoyed.

What were you taking pictures of?

I tried to explain - calmly at first. I'm a photographer. I saw these abandoned buildings. I was curious. I didn't cross any fence lines. Nobody was around.

But he cut me off.

You can't take pictures here, he said firmly.

Now, this is where I should have just nodded and left.

But noooo - I had to make a point.

The buildings are empty, I said. *They're abandoned. What exactly am I not supposed to see?*

He crossed his arms, his patience clearly thinning.

You need to delete the photos.

Cue my mom rolling up slowly in our truck. I could feel her gaze drilling into me - silent but screaming:

Yo ass going to jail, and we out here in the middle of nodamnwhere.

Pissed but cornered, I started deleting photos in front of him. But that wasn't enough.

He wanted to see the empty camera - scroll through and confirm there was nothing left.

Are you freak'n kidding me?

I complied, still steaming inside.

He finally let me go, and I climbed back into our truck, hot as fish grease.

We didn't say a word until we were off the property.

Then... my mom burst out laughing.

"Yo ass was gonna go to jail."

"And it ain't shit I could do to get you out –

annnd we not stopping no. damn. more."

I Didn't Cancel My Vacation: It Was Mine to Take

We didn't need a plan. We had the road, and it was ours to explore.

We pretty much take the same time off every year - mid-spring, mid-fall, and our birthdays. The air is lighter, the roads less crowded, and it's the sweet spot between *"too cold" and "I'm melting."* So, those are our travel windows. We always know when, just not always where.

This time, we had five days to play with, including a weekend. But for reasons I still can't recall, we were stuck in travel limbo. Couldn't decide where to go - or even if we should go. It got so bad, I considered turning the days back in. Secretly, I had already started nesting - mentally preparing to stay home.

Meanwhile, my mom was off helping a friend with house projects, due back the day my break began. The night before I called her....

Me: *I still have the time off... haven't turned it in yet.*
Mary: *And?*
Me: *I don't want to stay home. Can we pull off a trip?*
Mary: *Pause. Let me check my accounts.*
Minutes later, she called back.
Mary: *Yeah. When are we leaving?*
Me: *Do you need anything from the house to pack?*
Mary: *Nope. I've got what I need. Just throw the 'essentials' in a bag.*

And just like that, we had a road trip.

No destination.

No real plan.

Just a general feeling.

We wanted to try and venture a little west of our normal jaunts.

As far west as we'd been was Texas – but we didn't want to go the southern route. Detroit floated as maybe. Not a hard yes, but enough of a compass point to get us moving.

And yeah, before you give me the side-eye - no, we hadn't booked any hotels.

Don't act surprised.

Hazard Ahead

I picked Mary up around 10 a.m. that Wednesday, and off we went. First stop was a quick pit stop in the mountains of Jefferson County to visit a friend. A short visit and a warm hello, then back on the road - still vaguely heading toward Detroit.

We drove into the night, winding our way through backroads until we realized it was nearly midnight, and we needed a place to sleep. I pulled up my hotel app and found a place in Hazard, Kentucky. No, it has no direct affiliation to the tv show.

The front desk clerk was kind enough to tip us off about the only open restaurant nearby that delivered. We ordered food, flopped on the beds, and started rethinking the whole Detroit idea. We were unsure about the terrain at that time of the year *(April)*. So... we pivoted - better safe than sorry.
Let's go northeast, I said.
Maine? Mom asked.

We'd always talked about doing that trip. It was our original plan when I scheduled the time off - It made sense.

Decision made, I booked a room in Lancaster, Pennsylvania to break the drive. Then, we ate and knocked out for the night.

Holler, if You Hear Me

We got up early and hit the road again. Not long into the drive, we saw these stunning rock formations and pulled off to snap some photos. Then back on the road until we passed one of those brown historical markers that read: *This way to Loretta Lynn's birthplace.*

Now, I'm a Loretta fan. My mom knew it. So of course, we made the detour.

We followed the signs through Van Lear, the small mining town Loretta Lynn called home, and found ourselves at the Webb family store. I didn't even know they had one - but then, why would I? The building was what I'd imagine for the area - wide plank wood floors worn soft with time, paint peeling like old postcards, snacks from another era, and Loretta and Crystal Gayle memorabilia everywhere. *(If you didn't know, Crystal Gayle is Loretta's baby sister-almost twenty years her junior.)*

The guy at the counter, a Webb relative, told us there was a tour about to leave for the family home.

Did we want in?

Absolutely.

We formed a convoy and climbed a narrow single-lane road through the woods to the top of the holler. The view was beautiful. The house looked as if it had been aged with fire - its wooden siding darkened like shou sugi ban cedar *(thank you, Chip and Joanna Gaines, for the drop of random knowledge).*

The yard was lush and green. In a pasture, a horse rolled happily in the grass - though he looked a little worse for wear, with a matted coat and a deep swayback, but spirits high.

Inside the house? A time warp. Quilts, wood stoves, books, furniture - all from another time. Loretta and Crystal's presence was everywhere. I was in my element. The space reminded me so much of my childhood home, it almost ached.

Eventually, we climbed back down the mountain, grabbed snacks at the store, and got back on the road toward Lancaster.

Loretta Lynn's Childhood Home

The Cork & A Village

Nine hours later, we landed in Lancaster, Pennsylvania. We stayed at the *Cork Factory Hotel* - an old cork-making plant, revitalized into a boutique hotel with historic bones and modern charm.

After breakfast the next morning, we were ready to head toward Salem, Massachusetts, when a sign caught our eye: *Amish Village*.

You already know what we did.

We parked and wandered through a museum-like time capsule of Amish living - hand-stitched quilts, hand-carved furniture, potbelly stoves, and outside in the workers shed, tools that took my mom right back to her childhood. She picked up items, showing me how she used them with her father. I just watched, quietly. These little memory moments - small but mighty - are the ones I love most.

Instead of digging deeper into Amish Country, we hit the road. Salem awaited.

WHAT WE FOUND ALONG THE WAY

Amish Village – Lancaster, Pa

Deadman's Curves and Audio Gold

By the time we crossed into Massachusetts, it was dark and stormy. Raining, foggy, winding mountain roads - kind of stormy. We were making our way to our hotel in Peabody - about fifteen minutes outside of Salem - but it felt like a Hitchcock movie.

Normally, Mary catches a nap. Not this time.

She was wide awake, seat pulled up to the dash, phone out, recording. Listening to the playback later was pure comedy. It sounded like an old radio show -you could hear us laughing, talking, cursing the curves.

Slow down! she shouted - though it was dressed up in much stronger language.

The curves were deep. With the rain, it was hard to see in front of us, forget about on the sides. We could only see as far as the headlights would allow. No other cars. Blackness everywhere. One side, rock - the mountain. The other - an abyss.

Eventually, we made it to the hotel, checked in, and called it a night.

Witches, Writers, and Weathered Souls

Salem was... something else.

We drove through, then circled back, parked and took off on foot to see what had caught our eye. First stop: the memorial for the Salem witch trials. A stone wall with the names of the twenty accused of witchery were etched into stone benches - names, execution methods, dates - surrounded a graveyard.

Solemn. Humbling. Important.

Nearby was a replica of the pillory - the head-and-hands contraption they used back then. Mary popped her head and hands in that thing like it meant nothing. I, on the other hand - much more reserved *(shocker)* - didn't even want to play like that. Hard pass. Some things I'm happy just to just see in a movie.

We wandered towards a wharf, pausing to window-shop before finding ourselves at the edge of the *Derby Wharf Light Station*. The wind howled, the wind – brisk, but still the view was worth it - quieter than I expected.

From there, we made our way to *The House of Seven Gables*. Dark grey with a deep red door - I imagine a nod to *The Scarlet Letter*. Inside, the past didn't feel distant. Nathaniel Hawthorne's world felt alive in those small rooms, with shadowed stairwells, creaking floorboards beneath our feet, and low ceilings that made every step feel deliberate.

When we stepped back out, we wandered up the street and settled on a stoop - just talking and recapping the day and laughing.

Then I had a thought. "Gloucester's nearby, right?"

So, we went. Long winding roads opened to breathtaking views of the sea. I had hoped to catch a whale watch, but the ships were docked - weather too rough. Then I saw a statue. The Fisherman's Memorial.

I pulled over. Mary stayed in the car - blistering cold had no hold on her that day. The sculpture looked just like the Gorton's fisherman. It honored those lost at sea. This memorial included the names of fisherman lost at sea. If you've seen *The Perfect Storm*, the crew of the *Andrea Gail* is listed there too.

It was quiet. Beautiful. Sobering.

Homebound

We tried to book a seaside room that night, but no luck. Everything was full. So, we made the decision to head back home as opposed to driving another 279 miles to Maine. Another time, we said.

We didn't make it to Maine. But by then, it didn't matter.

So, we got back in the car and pointed ourselves home.

What mattered was that we made memories. We said yes when it would've been easier to stay home. And we made space - for lots of detours, loads of discovery, and for each other.

That's the thing about road trips: the destination is rarely the reward.

The reward is what you learn while the wheels are turning.

Gloucester Fisherman Memorial

(Trust the Gorton's Fisherman)

To My Mom

I remember on one of our trips, you told me you had always dreamed of being a flight attendant.

You wanted to get out of Halifax County (NC) because you knew there had to be something more - something bigger than what was expected of you.

You wanted to travel, to see the world, to live a life of adventure and new experiences.

You couldn't pursue that dream back then. Life, family, and responsibilities had other plans for you.

Thinking back, I can see now that's why you never said no to any opportunity that was presented to me.

You made it happen - somehow.

And ever since, every opportunity I've had, I've tried to turn it into something real - something **we** could share.

These small getaways, our road trips, our travels to Canada and Italy - they weren't just vacations.

They were pieces of a life you once imagined for yourself, lived out loud and together.

In my own way, I was giving you a taste of the world you once hoped to see.

And now, looking back, I realize those moments were and are **my thank you - my love letter to you.**

All the cheeky grins, the cussings out, the can-can dances -

they're engraved in my mind and are most definitely captured on file for all posterity – lol.

It's all of those things and so much more that just make me so proud and fill me with such joy and laughter.

This book, too, is part of that letter.

A tribute to the quiet strength and softness you've shown me, to the laughter and light you bring to every space we share. I hope others feel and can visualize that love in these pages. I hope they're reminded to

hold close the ones they love –

the ones who protect them –

and the ones who dreamt quietly while pushing them forward.

You've given me so much, Mommie – and I just wanted to give a little something back.

I love you.

Closing Words: The Road We Made Our Own

It was during a conversation with my friend Shumara - someone who knows my work, my ways, and my travel history - that she said something I hadn't considered.

She told me: *Cathy, you know... this feels like a modern-day take on the Green Book.*

That description was powerful. It hit, and it sat with me for a bit. I hadn't set out to write anything even remotely close to that. In fact, it had never crossed my mind. But the longer I thought about it, the more I understood the connection and relevance. She was right.

When I brought it to my mom, she pondered for a moment, then gave Mara her props.

The Negro Motorist Green Book was once a guide to freedom on the American road. I even have a *"modernized"* copy in my collection. It was a companion for Black travelers - listing towns, hotels, and cafés where one could stop without fear. Places where you could breathe a little easier. Where dignity was not stripped away. It was more than a book. It was a map of what-if, where-to, and do we dare.

The need for such a guide eventually faded. Yet the truth behind it - the human need to know where we will be welcomed, where we will be seen, where we can simply *be* - has not.

What We Found Along the Way became our own kind of map. Not made of addresses and mileage, but of moments. Each story creating a landscape.

My mom has always wanted to hang a wall map with pins marking every place we've been. And maybe this book became my way of doing that - only instead of pins, we marked the moments. The ones that shaped us. The ones that made us laugh. The ones that taught us something we didn't know we needed to learn. Each detour, each mile, answering those earlier questions

We began these journeys as a means to just to get out of the house and to learn more about the places we'd been adding to our *"lists"* - evolving into moments of meaning we shared together. But somewhere between the markers and the miles, I realized we were charting the map of us - mother and daughter - claiming the road in our own way.

We weren't necessarily looking for anything. But we always found something that mattered. And maybe that is the true purpose of any map:

not to promise perfection - but to guide you toward what will

shape you

hold you

change you

This is our Green Book. Our proof that the road is wide open - and ours to claim.

What will you find along the way?

About the Authors

I'm Cathy - born with a story already unfolding.

Delivered by my grandmother's hands in the back room of the house my grandfather built, the day after my mom's birthday in Tillery, North Carolina.

I've always had people in my corner, pushing me to try, to explore, to step outside the lines.

Maybe that's why I've always had a bit of a **RebelSoul** - going left when others went right. That same audacity has taken me across stages and continents: from concert photography to art exhibits in Italy and England; to starting a lifestyle blog with one of my best friends; bringing community together through DEI work; having my photos featured in the Little Brother documentary *May the Lord Watch*, and now co-authoring a book with my bestest friend, my mother.

I love stories. Whether I'm telling them through a camera lens or through words on a page, this feels like my heart's true work.

My mom, Mary, is the second of four children - born and raised in Tillery, NC. A quiet dreamer whose plans were gently put on pause when her family needed her most.

She spent decades serving Halifax County Schools (NC), all while raising me - sometimes working two or three jobs at once. She did what was necessary so I could dream without limits, making sure I always had what I needed - not wanted, but needed.

She's the kind of woman who says *Yes* when it matters most.

The kind who packs a bag without hesitation.

Her love has always shown up through action - through sacrifice, through presence, through that steady, unshakeable belief in possibility.

It is because of her that I learned the value of hard work and the importance of following your passion, even when the path isn't clear.

As mother and daughter, we've always shared a bond - but it's grown even stronger over time.

Together, we've covered countless miles - some just down the road, others across the ocean - collecting the stories and photographs that became *What We Found Along the Way*.

It's our first book together, but honestly, it's been in the making for a lifetime.

WHAT WE FOUND ALONG THE WAY

Cathy R. Foreman and Mary Foreman –
1977 - Dawson Elementary School

Thank You Note

What We Found Along the Way wasn't just the destinations - it was each other. Carry that forward.

Thank you for spending time with our stories and being a part of our journey. Writing, much like life, is a process with its own ebbs and flows. There are moments of clarity and moments of frustration - but the key is not to let the hard parts take you down. Step back, reassess, and let the words come naturally.

Editing is its own beast. The most important part is simply getting the words down. Don't worry about perfection in the first draft - otherwise, you risk getting stuck and never moving forward. Write or dictate it out, then go back and shape it. Even in the hardest stretches, you'll see progress, and that's worth celebrating.

We want to leave you with a challenge… **be spontaneous.**

Hit the road with no destination in mind, travel the back roads, stop along the way. Pay attention to those historical markers and billboards, take pictures, and enjoy getting lost on purpose. You'll be amazed at what you see, and what you find.

We hope you enjoyed our memories. Now go make your own. And when you do, share a memory with us - and if a specific memory or the relationship between my mom and me touched you, we'd love to hear about it. We also encourage you to leave a review so others can join this journey.

Be Blessed and Safe Travels

Cathy and Mary

www.ingramcontent.com/pod-product-compliance
Lightning Source LLC
Chambersburg PA
CBHW030449100526
44580CB00002B/45